D1503248

We Are Women

Celebrating Our Wit and Grit

June Cotner & Barb Mayer

Andrews McMeel
Publishing®

a division of Andrews McMeel Universal

We Are Women

Andrews McMeel Publishing
a division of Andrews McMeel Universal
1130 Walnut Street, Kansas City, Missouri 64106

www.andrewsmcmeel.com

16 17 18 19 20 TEN 10 9 8 7 6 5 4 3 2 1

ISBN: 978-1-4494-7170-5

Library of Congress Control Number: 2015950234

ATTENTION: SCHOOLS AND BUSINESSES

Andrews McMeel books are available at quantity discounts with bulk purchase
for educational, business, or sales promotional use. For information,
please e-mail the Andrews McMeel Publishing Special Sales Department:
specialsales@amuniversal.com.

Book design by Holly Ogden
Cover photo: N.d.; State Archives of Florida, Florida Memory; *www.floridamemory.com/items/show/12414*
Back cover photo: 1940s; *www.dailyfailcenter.com/83881*

For our mothers

Betty Elvira Baxter
1925–1961
(June's mother)

Helen "June" Mayer
1927–1980
(Barb's mother)

"Look upon this face, and know
that I was a person, here, in this time and place,
and I was happy."

WRITTEN ON THE BACK OF AN EARLY TWENTIETH-CENTURY WOMAN'S PHOTOGRAPH

ALSO BY JUNE COTNER

Note to Readers

From June: I enjoy browsing through vintage greeting cards, especially those featuring photos of women, and I found myself wondering one day what kind of lives these women led. What were their hopes and fears—their dreams and aspirations? Over time, this curiosity evolved into an idea for a book that would feature vintage photos paired with inspiring and sometimes humorous quotes—one that would remind readers how women's character and strength have endured through time.

I asked my dear friend (and photographer) Barb Mayer to coauthor this book. Together we studied thousands of images and quotations. Our aim was to create a book that would resonate emotionally with readers, while adding a touch of humor. Our final selection of photos, ranging in date from 1902 to 1960, offer relatable reflections on contemporary life.

To ensure that the book would appeal to younger women, we ran the samples by Kirsten, my thirty-six-year-old daughter, and Laura, my twenty-seven-year-old assistant. Kirsten was moved by the women in the photos, commenting that they inspired her to go out and live a full life just as they did. To Laura, the images were a reminder that women have always been strong, exciting, fun, and fascinating, and that it was our legacy to continue the tradition.

Your adventure awaits! I hope you will be uplifted and delighted by these photos that capture female fun and togetherness while embodying the best of the human spirit.

From Barb: When my friend June Cotner asked me to coauthor *We Are Women*, I accepted without hesitation. Researching vintage photos was a dream come true for me. As a child, I spent countless hours poring through my Dad's photo albums, trying to imagine the life my ancestors led—a life that seemed so different from mine.

The more photos June and I found for the book, the more I had to change my notion that women from the past were staid and serious. Within these old photos was a whole new world of fascinating females—women working out at the gym, women pumping gas, women sitting proudly on motorcycles. Dreamers and schemers, the women in these pictures were a far cry from the portraits I'd seen in thrift shops and family photo albums.

My research became a compulsion as I continued to uncover parts of history I knew nothing about. There were the Women Airforce Service Pilots (WASPs), women trained to fly military aircraft in World War II (p. 30). There was the Anti-Flirt Club, a group dedicated to warding off the unwanted advances of predatory men (p. 9). There were women who delighted in just being different—they were daring, innovative, and, most of all, fun-loving. Many were pioneers who paved the way for later generations of women to enter fields that were traditionally dominated by men.

As you page through the book, I hope that you are moved, as I was, by the spirit and tenacity of these women, our ancestors.

Happy reading!

If you want anything said, ask a man.
If you want anything done, ask a woman.

Margaret Thatcher

If you obey all the rules, you miss all the fun.

Katharine Hepburn

Call it a clan, call it a network,
call it a tribe, call it a family.
Whatever you call it, whoever you are,
you need one.

Jane Howard

Some people think having large breasts makes a woman stupid.

Actually, it's quite the opposite:
a woman having large breasts makes men stupid.

Rita Rudner

I'm not offended by all the dumb blonde jokes
because I know I'm not dumb—
and I'm also not blonde.

Dolly Parton

One is not born a woman,
but rather becomes one.

Simone de Beauvoir

Our deepest fear is not that we are inadequate.
Our deepest fear is that we are powerful beyond measure.

Marianne Williamson

I tried being normal,
but I didn't like it.

Author unknown

Don't fall for the slick, dandified cake eater—
the unpolished gold of a real man
is worth more than the gloss of a lounge lizard.

Rule #8 of the Anti-Flirt Club

FOUNDED IN WASHINGTON, D.C. (1923)

There is eternal influence and power in motherhood.

Julie B. Beck

Love's greatest gift is its ability
to make everything it touches sacred.

Barbara De Angelis

As you move through life,
leave a wake of kindness.

Margaret Hale

There's power in looking silly

and not caring that you do.

Amy Poehler

When my kids become wild and unruly,
I use a nice, safe playpen.

When they're finished, I climb out.

Erma Bombeck

Families are like fudge—

mostly sweet with a few nuts.

Author unknown

Life isn't a matter of milestones, but of moments.

Rose Kennedy

That it will never come again is what makes life so sweet.

Emily Dickinson

Love is like pi—natural, irrational,

and very important.

Lisa Hoffman

Every man I meet wants to protect me.
I can't figure out what from.

Mae West

The best thing to hold on to in life is each other.

Audrey Hepburn

Each friend represents a world in us,
a world possibly not born until they arrive,
and it is only by this meeting that a new world is born.

Anaïs Nin

I love you not only for what you are,
but for what I am when I am with you.

Elizabeth Barrett Browning

Love at first sight is easy to understand;

it's when two people have been looking at each other
for a lifetime that it becomes a miracle.

Amy Bloom

Women complain about PMS,
but I think of it as the only time of the month
when I can be myself.

Roseanne Barr

A girl can wait for the right man to come along,

but in the meantime that still doesn't mean
she can't have a wonderful time
with all the wrong ones.

Cher

Each day comes bearing its own gifts.
Untie the ribbons.

Ruth Ann Schabacker

Life is so endlessly delicious.

Ruth Reichl

Today's preparation determines tomorrow's achievement.

Author unknown

Life without a little risk is not
an adventure darling,
it's a darn shame.

Leigh Standley

It's a great satisfaction knowing that
for a brief point in time you made a difference.

Irene Natividad

The purpose of life, after all, is to live it, to taste experience to the utmost,
to reach out eagerly and without fear for newer and richer experience.

Eleanor Roosevelt

31

Your children make it impossible to regret your past.
They're its finest fruits.

Anna Quindlen

While we try to teach our children all about life,
our children teach us what life is all about.

Author unknown

Spend your life doing strange things with weird people.

Author unknown

There is a direct correlation
between the level of happiness in one's life
and the amount of silliness they allow into it.

Leigh Standley

Whatever your cause,
have fun along the way.

June Cotner

What you do makes a difference,
and you have to decide
what kind of difference you want to make.

Jane Goodall

Sometimes courage is the quiet voice
at the end of the day saying,
"I will try again tomorrow."

Mary Anne Radmacher

Sometimes, reaching out and taking someone's hand
is the beginning of a journey.
At other times, it is allowing another to take yours.

Vera Nazarian

Friends are like walls.
Sometimes you lean on them,
and sometimes it's good just knowing they are there.

Author unknown

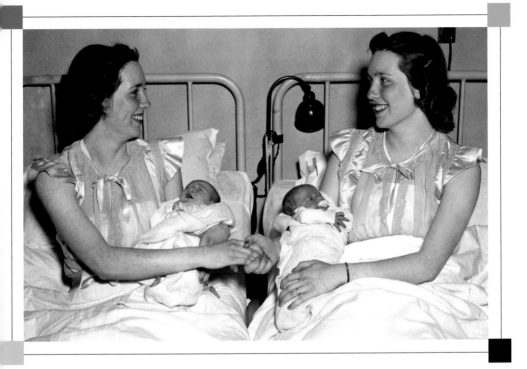

Side by side, or miles apart,
we are sisters connected by heart.

Author unknown

Every day each of us wakes up, reaches into drawers and closets,
pulls out a costume for the day and proceeds to dress
in a style that can only be called preposterous.

Mary Schmich

Normal is in the eye of the beholder.

Whoopi Goldberg

The question isn't who's going to let me;

it's who is going to stop me.

Ayn Rand

Let's dare to be ourselves,
for we do that better than anyone else can.

Shirley Briggs

I figure if a girl wants to be a legend,
she should just go ahead and be one.

Calamity Jane

Life will change without our permission.
It's our attitude that will determine the ride.

Author unknown

You've only got three choices in life—
give up, give in, or give it all you've got.

Author unknown

I want it all

and I want it delivered.

Bette Midler

When was the last time you did something for the first time?

Author unknown

Never take a shortcut in life. Take the long route,
because you pick up more experiences on the way.

Author unknown

Remember, we all stumble, every one of us.
That's why it's a comfort to go hand in hand.

Emily Kimbrough

Do what makes you happy, be with who makes you smile,
laugh as much as you breathe,
and love as long as you live.

Rachel Ann Nunes

Ask questions. Stay curious.

It's much more important to be interested than to be interesting.

Jane Fonda

If you want to accomplish the goals of your life,
you have to begin with the spirit.

Oprah Winfrey

Our perfect companions
never have fewer than four feet.

Colette

Think P. I. G.—that's my motto.
P stands for Persistence, I stands for Integrity, and G stands for Guts.
These are the ingredients for a successful business and a successful life.

Linda Chandler

You can make it, but it's easier
if you don't have to do it alone.

Betty Ford

A man's got to do what a man's got to do.
A woman must do what he can't.

Rhonda Hansome

Even in the familiar there can be surprise and wonder.

Tierney Gearon

Why should we all dress after the same fashion?
The frost never paints my windows twice alike.

Lydia Maria Child

Sometimes you don't need words to feel better;
you just need the nearness of your dog.

Natalie Lloyd

Simplicity is the keynote of all true elegance.

Coco Chanel

The future belongs to those who believe
in the beauty of their dreams.

Eleanor Roosevelt

Never doubt that a small group
of thoughtful, committed people can change the world.
Indeed, it is the only thing that ever has.

Margaret Mead

True friends are like diamonds—

bright, beautiful, valuable, and always in style.

Nicole Richie

Find ecstasy in life;
the mere sense of living is joy enough.

Emily Dickinson

Anybody can be cool—
but awesome takes practice.

Lorraine Peterson

Trust in what you love, continue to do it,
and it will take you where you need to go.

Natalie Goldberg

I've learned that people will forget what you said,
people will forget what you did,
but people will never forget how you made them feel.

Maya Angelou

PHOTO CREDITS

Grateful acknowledgment is made to the rights holders and licensing agencies for the use of the following material. Every effort has been made to contact original sources. If notified, the publishers will be pleased to rectify an omission in future editions. Many thanks to Flickr: The Commons (*www.flickr.com/commons*) for providing access to the photos marked with asterisks. For a complete list of photo credits and historical details, please visit *www.barbmayer.com.*

Cover: N.d.; State Archives of Florida, Florida Memory; *www.floridamemory.com/items/show/12414*

page 1: 1944; Oregon State University Special Collections and Archives #HC972; *scarc.library.oregonstate.edu*

page 2: 1921; Isobel Dawson photo collection

page 3: 1927; Het Leven; Dutch National Archives, Spaarnestad Collection #SFA002009694; *www.spaarnestadphoto.nl*

page 4: N.d.; Barb Mayer photo collection; *www.barbmayer.com*

page 5: 1920s; *www.flickr.com/photos/34692952@N06/3229262909*

page 6: 1919; A. H. Poole Studio; National Library of Ireland*; *catalogue.nli.ie/Record/vtls000593335*

page 7: 1935; Fox Photos; Getty Images Prestige HB5492-001; *www.gettyimages.com*

page 8: 1939; *www.huffingtonpost.com/2013/04/04/dot-robinson-vintage-biker-el-knucklehead_n_3016702.html*

page 9: 1923; National Photo Co.; Library of Congress; *www.loc.gov/pictures/item/npc2007007777*

page 10: 1920; John P. Troy; Cornell University Library, Rare and Manuscript Collection*, #23-2-749, RT-S-16; *he-photos.library.cornell.edu/image.php?record=16*

page 11: c1910; Henry Essenhigh Corke; © Royal Photographic Society, National Media Museum, Science & Society Picture Library*, all rights reserved; *www.nationalmediamuseum.org.uk*

page 12: c1960; Ralph Walker; Courtesy of Missouri State Archives*, Image #CID_057-003; *www.sos.mo.gov/mdh*

page 13: 1929; *www.thesilentmovieblog.wordpress.com/category/photo-gallery*

page 14: N.d.; Flickr Vintage Postcard Images; *www.flickr.com/photos/takeabreakwithme/3106020624*

page 15: 1922; Isobel Dawson photo collection

page 16: 1922; National Photo Co.; Library of Congress; *www.loc.gov/pictures/item/npc2007005677*

page 17: 1944; National Archives and Records Administration, #520646; *www.archives.gov*

page 18: 1946; Smithsonian Institution Archives*, Image #90-105; *www.siarchives.si.edu*

page 19: 1931; Austrian Archives; Getty Images, Gamma-Keystone Collection, #466703383; *www.gettyimages.com*

page 20: 1940s; Shutterstock, Everett Collection #92590018; *www.shutterstock.com*

page 21: 1949; Mitchell Library, State Library of New South Wales, PXA 584; *www.sl.nsw.gov.au*

page 22: N.d.; Sven Türck; The Royal Library, Denmark* #turck_22013; *www.kb.dk/images/billed/2010/okt/billeder/object67317/en*

page 23: 1935; Einar Erici; Swedish National Heritage Board*, EE0045; *kmb.raa.se*

page 24: N.d.; Bain News Service; Library of Congress; *www.loc.gov/pictures/item/2002697718*

page 25: 1944; Jim Fitzpatrick; National Library of Australia*, #669443; *www.nla.gov.au/nla.pic-an24340443*

page 26: 1929; Isobel Dawson photo collection

page 27: c1903; Miles Bros.; Library of Congress, National Photo Co.; *www.loc.gov/pictures/item/2002716008*

page 28: 1936; Harris and Ewing; Library of Congress; *www.loc.gov/pictures/item/hec2013003527*

page 29: 1948; Joseph Steinmetz; State Archives of Florida, Florida Memory; *www.floridamemory.com/items/show/252534*

page 30: 1943; U.S. National Archives; *www.archives.gov*

page 31: 1928; Southern Methodist University, Central University Libraries, DeGolyer Library*; *digitalcollections.smu.edu/cdm/ref/collection/jtx/id/622*

page 32: 1939; Dorothea Lange; Library of Congress, Farm Security Administration; *www.loc.gov/pictures/item/fsa2000004496/PP*

page 33: 1941; Alfred Eisenstaedt; Getty Images, LIFE Picture Collection, #53378644; *www.gettyimages.com*

page 34: 1922; National Photo Co.; Library of Congress; *www.loc.gov/pictures/item/npc2007006608*

page 35: 1920s; National Photo Co.; Library of Congress; *www.loc.gov/pictures/item/93505158*

page 36: 1940s; *www.vintag.es/2013/06/skate-to-work-save-gas-ca-1940s.html*

page 37: c1915; Bain News Service; Library of Congress; *www.loc.gov/pictures/item/ggb2005019656*

page 38: 1938; Russell Lee; Library of Congress, U.S. Farm Security Administration; *www.loc.gov/pictures/item/fsa1997023203/PP*

page 39: 1909; Library of Congress; *www.loc.gov/pictures/item/2002706661*

page 40: c1955; Gerald R. Massie; Courtesy of the Missouri State Archives*, #CID_019_111; *www.sos.mo.gov/mdh*

page 41: 1939; Harris and Ewing; Library of Congress; *www.loc.gov/pictures/item/hec2009013324*

page 42: 1930; National Library of Ireland*, Poole Photographic Collection, NLI Ref P_WP_3785; *www.nli.ie/digital-photographs.aspx*

page 43: 1944; Australian War Memorial Collection; *www.awm.gov.au/collection/140486*

page 44: 1920s; *www.vintag.es/2012/02/freaky-retro-photos.html*

page 45: c1925; Harald Østmoe photo collection

page 46: c1930; Wikimedia Commons; *https://commons.wikimedia.org/wiki/File:Springfield_cowgirls.jpg*

page 47: c1910; Charles Elliott; Courtesy of the Missouri State Archives*, Image #MS330_619; *www.sos.mo.gov/mdh*

page 48: 1928; Harris and Ewing; Library of Congress; *www.loc.gov/pictures/item/hec2013005129*

page 49: c1920; *www.pinterest.com/pin/216665432048839548*

page 50: 1924; National Photo Co.; Library of Congress; *www.loc.gov/pictures/item/npc2007010442*

page 51: 1925; National Photo Co.; Library of Congress; *www.loc.gov/pictures/item/npc2007012972*

page 52: c1935; State Library of Queensland*, Record #80651; *www.slq.qld.gov.au/resources/picture-queensland*

page 53: N.d.; Het Leven; Dutch National Archives*, Spaarnestad Collection #SFA001008525; *www.spaarnestadphoto.nl*

page 54: 1940s; *themusesings.wordpress.com*

page 55: 1908; J. L. Blessing; Wikimedia Commons; *www.commons.wikimedia.org/wiki/File:Ah-Weh-Eyu.jpg*

page 56: N.d.; Willem Van de Poll; Dutch National Archives*, Van de Poll Collection, Image #189-0240; *www.gahetna.nl*

page 57: c1916; White Studio; Library of Congress; *www.loc.gov/pictures/item/2011660905*

page 58: 1918; War Department; U.S. National Archives, #533758; *https://research.archives.gov/id/533758*

page 59: 1927; National Photo Co.; Library of Congress; *www.loc.gov/pictures/item/94508166*

page 60: 1929; *www.golbis.com/pin/post-deystvitelno-redkih-fotografiy-2/#.VWlUvUbeMxw*

page 61: 1921; Library of Congress; *www.loc.gov/pictures/item/2008681153*

page 62: 1925; National Photo Co.; Library of Congress; *www.loc.gov/pictures/item/npc2007013418*

page 63: 1933; Willem Van de Poll; Dutch National Archives*; *beeldbank.nationaalarchief.nl/na:col1:dat428623*

page 64: 1902; Fitz W. Guerin; Library of Congress; *www.loc.gov/pictures/item/2003677242*

page 65: 1920; National Photo Co.; Library of Congress; *www.loc.gov/pictures/item/npc2007001204*

page 66: 1950s; *www.vintag.es/2014_05_01_archive.html*

page 67: N.d.; State Archives of Florida, Florida Memory; *www.floridamemory.com/items/show/12414*

page 68: 1940s; *www.dailyfailcenter.com/83881*

page 69: 1948; *www.sunvalleymag.com/Sun-Valley-Magazine/Winter-2012/75-Years-of-Sun-Valley*

page 70: N.d.; Barb Mayer photo collection; *www.barbmayer.com*

ABOUT THE AUTHORS

June Cotner is the author of thirty-three books, including the best-selling *Graces* and *Bedside Prayers*. Her books altogether have sold more than one million copies and have been featured in many national publications, including *USA Today*, *Better Homes and Gardens*, *Woman's Day*, and *Family Circle*. June has appeared on national television and radio programs.

June's latest love and avocation is giving presentations on adopting prisoner-trained shelter dogs. In 2011, she adopted Indy, a chocolate Lab/Doberman mix (a LabraDobie!), from the Freedom Tails program in Aberdeen, Washington. She and Indy have appeared on the television shows *AM Northwest* (Portland, Oregon) and *New Day Northwest* (Seattle, Washington).

A graduate of the University of California at Berkeley, June is the mother of two grown children and lives in Poulsbo, Washington, with her husband. Her hobbies include yoga, hiking, and playing with her two grandchildren.

For more information, please visit June's website at www.junecotner.com.

Barb Mayer is a frequent contributor to the anthologies of June Cotner, as well as an award-winning photographer. Born in London, England, she relocated to Canada, then to America, developing along the way a zest for travel and foreign culture.

She worked for many years as a computer analyst but now devotes her time to writing, photography, and visiting her four children and grandchildren. She divides her year among three diverse places: the Pacific Northwest; Oahu, Hawaii; and Palombara-Sabina, Italy, where she shares a small country house with her partner.

For more about Barb Mayer, please visit her website at www.barbmayer.com.